MW01108904

Discovering
Dark
Matter

PHILIP WOLNY

ROSEN
PUBLISHING

New York

Published in 2015 by The Rosen Publishing Group, Inc.
29 East 21st Street, New York, NY 10010

Library of Congress Cataloging-in-Publication Data

Wolny, Philip, author.
Discovering dark matter/Philip Wolny.—First edition.
    pages cm.—(The scientist's guide to physics)
Includes bibliographical references and index.
ISBN 978-1-4777-8004-6 (library bound)
1. Dark matter (Astronomy)—Juvenile literature. I. Title.
QB791.3.W65 2015
523.1'126—dc23

                                                        2014015412

Manufactured in China

Contents

INTRODUCTION

Vera Rubin was busy at work, watching the skies. It was the late 1960s, and the rest of her peers at the Department of Terrestrial Magnetism in Washington, D.C., seemed to be chasing quasars, which are bright, faraway, and mysterious objects similar to stars. Not wanting to follow the crowd, Rubin had taken another path. The astronomer, working with her colleague W. Kent Ford, was observing the movements of stars in the Andromeda galaxy, tracking how they rotated within Andromeda itself.

They looked at these stars in a way that no one else had been able to before. Ford had developed an improved version of a tool called a spectrograph, or

Vera Rubin is perhaps the most important and influential astronomer in the modern era to advance and popularize the theories surrounding dark matter.

spectrometer. It helped them see patterns invisible to the naked human eye. With it, they could also record light patterns much more quickly than earlier scientists. Rubin knew they would be able to examine star rotations that were farther from the central bulge of the galaxy than any other researchers before them.

There was one problem that had not stopped nagging at Rubin since the beginning of their experiments, however. She had expected to see the outer stars of the Andromeda rotating more slowly than those closer to its center. Mapped on a graph, this "rotation curve" should have been similar to other orbiting bodies. In our solar system, for example, planets with bigger orbits—like Uranus and Neptune—travel slower. Earth moves around the sun more quickly than these outer planets. But as they mapped rotation in the Andromeda galaxy, Rubin and Ford found a flat line. There was no curve. This meant that all the stars moved at the same rate.

Rubin and Ford's discovery called into question what scientists understood as the nature of the universe itself. Decades earlier, scientists working with more basic instruments, such as Fritz Zwicky in the 1930s, had noticed similar phenomena. The laws of physics first conceived of by Isaac Newton and later applied to the movements of galaxies and stars, sometimes called Newtonian physics, held that the masses and distances of rotating objects would determine their motions in predictable ways. The gravity of a spiral galaxy would be concentrated at its center. Therefore, stars nearer to the center would move faster than those further away due to gravitational pull. But the difference between the visible matter they witnessed and the unexpected behavior of the stars they observed meant they were on to something entirely new. There had to be some other kind of matter exerting gravitational forces on the stars that were further away from the center of a spiral galaxy.

These new and unusual findings from Rubin and Ford would lead to a worldwide search. Decades were spent on the search for a mysterious substance that may comprise most of the universe but which we know very little about: dark matter.

With improvements in the tools available for research, scientists have been able to approach the study of this mysterious substance from many angles. Astrophysicists look for evidence among the stars. Particle physicists search in objects millions of times smaller than what we can see with a regular microscope. Today, billions of dollars are invested in dark matter research projects worldwide. At this very moment, there are many scientists trying to unlock the secrets of dark matter.

WHAT IS THE UNIVERSE MADE OF?

Chapter 1

Throughout history, people have looked to the stars with amazement and wonder. Ancient civilizations, like the Greeks, Egyptians, and Chinese, made up stories to explain what they observed in the night sky. It was their attempt to explain the universe. As technology was developed, stories turned into scientific investigation and experimentation. It helped to shape the study of physics, astronomy, and astrophysics. These investigations help us better understand how the universe works. But after all this time, the most important question still remains: "What is the universe made of?"

Scientists have grappled with this question for hundreds of years. They aim to discover how the various parts of the universe behave. What is matter, really? And how can we understand something that we can't see? Scientists continually develop new ideas and test their theories. Theories are expanded and developed with each new discovery. Despite all we know about the universe today, we will know even more tomorrow.

THE UNIVERSE THEN AND NOW

Many ancient peoples developed systems of astronomy tied closely to their religious beliefs. These explained in a logical fashion what they saw in the night sky, while remaining true to their faith. The universe as they saw it included the planets of our

Shown here is a replica of a codex, or folding book, of the Maya, one of several advanced ancient civilizations whose science aimed to explain the universe.

solar system, the sun and the moon, and distant stars. Often, these were believed to be divine beings, such as gods and goddesses. For example, the mythology of the Maya people of southern Mexico and northern Central America included a conflict between the sun and the moon, which helped them explain why one would disappear when the other one appeared. In these early systems, Earth was the center of the universe, with these divine beings affecting humanity.

As early peoples observed the sky, they began to identify patterns of movement. They developed tools and instruments that helped them live and work. Farmers used the seasons to plan their crops. The stars aided sailors in navigating the seas. Ancient scientists learned more about the universe. One example of a helpful tool was the astrolabe. It was created in ancient Greece around 150 BCE. It measures distances on land and at sea using the angles of heavenly bodies in relation to the observer.

Tools continued to improve, and in 1609, Galileo Galilei, the famous Italian scientist, revolutionized astronomy with the telescope. With it, he observed previously unseen stars and got closer views of the moon and Jupiter's moons. For the first time, Galileo could see that the moon had a rough surface.

Over the centuries, ever more powerful telescopes and sophisticated technologies such as computers allowed scientists to better measure the

The ultrapowerful Hubble Space Telescope is one of the few pieces of equipment that has contributed a great deal to humanity's understanding of the universe.

properties of space and understand the objects in it. But for years, observations could only be made from Earth's surface. Science was limited by location. Additionally, images were distorted by Earth's atmosphere. Then the Hubble Space Telescope was developed. The Hubble is an orbiting telescope. It was launched by a space shuttle in 1990 and is still operational. Finally, scientists could see without the distortion caused by Earth's light and atmosphere.

Hubble's high resolution images have given us a clearer view of our universe.

Is What You See, What You Get?

For a very long time, research centered on the celestial bodies that could be seen with the human eye or with simple telescopes. These included the billions of stars that made up the various galaxies much like Earth's own, the Milky Way. This combined collection of objects in space is called the observable universe. It was taken for granted that the universe was made up of regular matter—that is, matter made up of protons, neutrons, and electrons. In different arrangements, these elements are the building blocks for all the materials in the universe. All living and nonliving matter, even the hot gases that make up stars, are built on these elements.

As technology improved what scientists could see, new theories developed. There were changes in what we understood about the origins of the universe and its size, age, and composition. Slowly, scientists discovered that the observable universe was not all there was. What they could see did not account for all the matter in the universe. So they began to look for things that they could not see. How? They looked

This illustration depicts a future merging of the Andromeda *(left)* and Milky Way *(right)* galaxies, which is predicted to occur within the next several billion years.

at how the objects that they could see behaved near unobservable objects.

An Expanding Universe

A little over a century ago, scientists believed that the universe did not change. In 1916, Albert Einstein changed that with his theory of relativity. The theory meant that what we knew of the universe was dependent on our frame of reference. The observable universe to someone standing still would be different to someone in motion. In fact, the only constant was the speed of light. Scientists began to see how space could expand or contract. This theory was difficult to accept, even for Einstein, despite it being based on his own work.

Dutch astronomer, physicist, and mathematician Willem de Sitter, bolstered by Einstein's theory, put forward another. He theorized that the universe was constantly expanding. Later investigations by Edwin Hubble in the late 1920s supported this view. Hubble helped convince much of the scientific community—Einstein included—that all the galaxies were moving away from each other. Furthermore, Hubble had deduced that galaxies further away from ours were moving away faster than closer ones. In the 1920s, Belgian priest and scientist Georges Lemaître and scientist Alexander Friedmann both proposed ideas for models of an expanding universe. By the 1940s, more scientists had refined this idea. Cosmologist Fred Hoyle gave it a catchy name: the big bang theory. According to the big bang theory, the universe began about fourteen billion years ago, when it was concentrated in a much smaller space. Imagine the universe on the head of a pin. Scientists theorized that at the time of the big bang, a thousand universes could fit on a pin. Lemaître called this tiny universe the primeval atom.

During the 1920s, Dutch scientist Jan Oort also aimed to figure out the amount of matter present in the Milky Way and the density of that matter. Density measures how much matter exists in a particular space. For example, a cubic foot of water vapor is less dense than a cubic foot of water because water particles are packed tighter in a space than water vapor particles. In particular, Oort and his peers were interested in how dense certain galaxies were. Connecting ideas about how the universe's density had changed over billions of years would give scientists clues about how the big bang worked. This is because different types of matter and particles had existed before the big bang than those that had been created by the changes in temperature and density that occurred just a few seconds after the big bang. Other types formed many centuries later, when temperatures dropped.

The density of the current universe, for example, is far lower than when all of that matter existed in Lemaître's primeval atom, right at the time of the big bang. With so much matter concentrated in such a tiny space, its particles contained so much energy that the universe was incredibly hot. It was billions of degrees

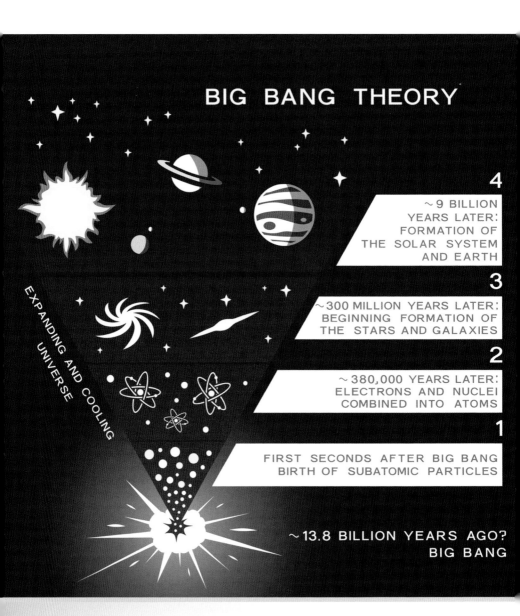

This infographic tracks the expansion of the universe from the very first seconds of the theoretical big bang to the present day.

Fahrenheit. That's hundreds of thousands of times hotter than the center of Earth's sun. Then it began expanding. And it continues to expand today. At only a minute old, the universe began to cool as it expanded in size. Cooling allowed new particles to form that had been impossible just seconds before. These new particles were protons and neutrons. A few minutes later, these had slowed down enough to combine and create atomic nuclei. Three hundred thousand years later, the universe had cooled to 3,000 degrees Celsius (5,432 degrees Fahrenheit), and now these nuclei were able to collect electrons and form the building blocks of matter as we know it. Normal matter is composed of protons and neutrons. This is called baryonic matter. But in astronomy, normal matter also includes electrons. Electrons are nonbaryonic. Since electrons in astronomical objects occur in extremely small quantities, they are essentially ignored. In astronomy, normal matter includes protons, neutrons, and tiny quantities of electrons. One of the properties of baryons is that they reflect light, which makes them visible. Vera Rubin, the astrophysicist mentioned earlier who studied the rotation of galaxies, realized that scientists made the mistake of taking this property of radiating light for granted. It was just an assumption. Like many assumptions made in science, however, later research would over time turn this idea about matter upside down, and Rubin would be a central player in doing so.

AGE OF EXPLORATION

Improving technology and theoretical innovation made the early part of the twentieth century an exciting one for scientists to explore the universe, even if the means did not exist for space travel. The discovery of galaxies beyond the Milky Way, the first detection of Pluto, and the early development of rocket fuel all helped usher in a century of exploration. New telescopes, including the first radio telescope, built by Grote Reber in 1937, extended the senses of scientists who scanned the heavens. Einstein's theory of relativity, first introduced in 1916, laid the groundwork for much of theoretical and practical physics and astrophysics. In this fertile environment of thought and innovation, it was perhaps inevitable that science would continue to make even greater advances.

A New Era of Understanding the Universe

The early twentieth century was an exciting time for new ideas in science, especially in physics, astronomy, and astrophysics. In 1931, Willem de Sitter was reported to have said, according to Robert Smith's book *Expanding Universe*, "Never in all the history of science has there been a period when new theories and hypotheses arose, flourished, and were abandoned in so quick succession as in the last fifteen or twenty years."

With ever-newer methods and instruments at their disposal, the scientists of the era made exciting discoveries. Edwin Hubble, in 1923, first identified galaxies outside the Milky Way, Earth's home galaxy. In 1926, Swedish researcher Bertil Lindblad observed that the Milky Way itself rotates around a central point. A few years later, Jan Oort observed the motions of stars and confirmed Lindblad's theory. Swiss astronomer and physicist Fritz Zwicky, however, challenged everyone's ideas about the makeup of the universe. Among other important work, Zwicky's observations on galactic motion questioned the belief that baryonic matter made up most of the substance of the universe. He was among the first to theorize on the mysterious stuff known as dark matter. This mystery would inspire and frustrate scientists studying the cosmos for the rest of the twentieth century and well into the twenty-first.

THE MISSING MATTER

Chapter

2

F ritz Zwicky is known for a variety of astronomical discoveries and theories. He spent most of his career with the California Institute of Technology in Pasadena, California, also known as Caltech. Zwicky developed a reputation for big ideas that many scientists found outlandish at first. Some were off the mark and were disproven. But many of his early theories were shown to be accurate through the work of his peers over several decades. In the book *Cosmic Horizons*, Zwicky was described as "the most unrecognized genius of twentieth-century astronomy."

One of Zwicky's accomplishments involved the phenomenon of supernovas. By the early 1920s, astronomers had begun to investigate the mysterious origin of cosmic rays. These were super-tiny particles, full of energy and shooting through space at nearly the speed of light. No one knew where they came from. Zwicky believed they were the result of supernovas. A supernova is an exploding star. The explosion of a star releases most of its matter out into the universe. It can create light millions of times more powerful than that of a normal star.

From Caltech's Mount Wilson Observatory, Zwicky discovered more supernovas than everyone who came before him combined. The more supernovas he saw, the more he thought about the nature of galaxies and how they grouped, or clustered together.

It was his observation of the Coma cluster that would set him on the path to an altogether new and exciting discovery. The Coma cluster is made up of about a thousand galaxies. Stick your thumb up in the air at arm's length. The space that your thumb takes up is about the area of the sky that the Coma cluster takes up as viewed from Earth. Zwicky had Caltech build him a Schmidt telescope 18 inches (46 centimeters) long that could view a wide-angle section of the night sky. It allowed him to observe large numbers of galaxies.

Astronomers and astrophysicists are able to tell much from differently colored wavelengths of light they detect in the universe using sensitive instruments.

THE DOPPLER SHIFT: MEASURING GALAXIES

Motions of individual galaxies are affected by the gravitational pull of their neighbors. They are also affected by the total gravitational force of the cluster as a whole. Zwicky carefully measured the movements of galaxies within the Coma cluster.

Zwicky's technique involved calculating their Doppler shifts. When you look at waves traveling on the surface of the ocean, you are seeing a Doppler shift. Doppler, named for Austrian physicist Christian Doppler, measures the change in the frequency of a wave. The frequency is measured relative to the source of the wave and the person observing it. Sound travels in waves. Think of a fire engine's alarm ringing out. As the fire engine approaches, the sound waves move

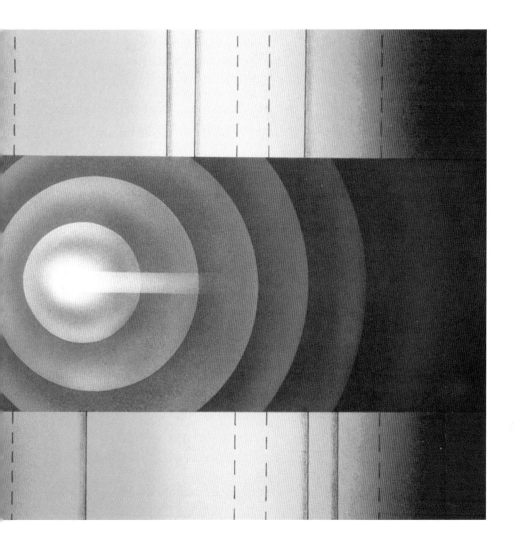

closer together relative to you, the observer. The sound has a high frequency. As the fire engine passes and moves away, the sound waves stretch out. The sound becomes lower in frequency.

Light also moves in waves in the form of light radiation, like starlight and sunlight. Its motion can be detected in a similar way to the sound of that fire engine. When a light source, like a star in a galaxy, moves toward the observer, it becomes bluer. When it moves away, it becomes redder. Using observatory telescopes, astronomers have been able to see how light on one side of a galaxy is blue shifted, while the other side is red shifted. These are how the human eye registers the differences in the frequencies of radiation from light sources. These different color shifts indicate how one side moves toward the observer on Earth, while the other moves away. Zwicky and others have analyzed combinations of these Doppler shifts to figure out the speeds of stars, galaxies, and other objects in space.

"Weighing" the Coma Cluster

Using his measurements, Zwicky was able to estimate the weight, or mass, of all the matter within the cluster. He used a standard unit of mass—one solar mass— which is about the mass of Earth's sun. Then he figured out the approximate number of galaxies in the cluster. He divided that total mass by the number of galaxies. Calculations showed that the Coma cluster had about fifty billion solar masses per galaxy. However, there was one problem: there was too little light.

Scientists use light output to give a good estimate of the total mass of a galaxy. The reason for that is that the main objects with any mass to them were light-generating stars. However, Zwicky's calculations showed that the Coma cluster had four hundred times more mass than the mass of its stars.

Zwicky also saw that the motion of the galaxies was far too fast to be accounted for by the visible matter. The stars and galaxies should have flown apart. Something was holding them together. Whatever it was produced its own gravitational fields but did not emit light. That's why Zwicky called it dark matter.

DOUBTING ZWICKY

Zwicky had some corroboration of his ideas from other scientists working at the time. One peer, Dutch astronomer Jan Oort, had also documented similar examples of "missing matter." Others were not so sure. In addition, Zwicky's reputation for being difficult did not help convince his colleagues. He was known to criticize and even insult fellow scientists and was rumored to be very demanding with his university students, too.

(continued on the next page)

Astrophysicist Fritz Zwicky explains how the planet Jupiter could get thrown out of its solar orbit in this photo taken at the California Institute of Technology, in Pasadena, California, in 1956.

(continued from the previous page)

Often, the time must be right for a new idea to take root with mainstream science, or it fails to stick. As Evalyn Gates wrote in *Einstein's Telescope*, "In spite of the catchy name, Zwicky's dark matter results were regarded with a healthy amount of skepticism by the astronomical community, which ignored them for the next 35 years or so."

WEIGHING THE EVIDENCE

At the time, the idea that most of the mass of the universe was invisible was revolutionary. Other scientists of their era distrusted Zwicky's and Oort's findings. Because many of the measurements and observations of the time were new and rough in their estimations, not everyone trusted the data to be accurate. Others believed that scientists did not know nearly enough about how galaxies behave to hold these observations up as proof of anything.

Additionally, some of Zwicky's other ideas were considered too unrealistic. However, later work by award-winning scientists owed much to Zwicky's initial ideas. In the academic quarterly *Beam Line*, Stephen M. Maurer wrote about Zwicky's maverick reputation, "When researchers talk about neutron stars, dark matter, and gravitational lenses, they all start the same way: 'Zwicky noticed this problem in the 1930s. Back then, nobody listened.'" But in the decade or so after Oort's and Zwicky's observations, evidence would continue to build.

In 1936, Sinclair Smith observed an entirely different mass of stars called the Virgo cluster. Smith observed thirty galaxies' velocity measurements. He drew pretty much the same conclusions as Zwicky.

Shown here is a set of galaxies that make up the Virgo cluster, which accounts for the part of the sky known to astronomers as the Virgo constellation.

Writing in the *Astrophysical Journal*, he noted that there was probably a "great mass of internebular material within the cluster." Smith's research suggested that this large amount of invisible matter probably held the galaxies together. The same year, Edwin Hubble stated that "the discrepancy seems to be real and is important" in his book, *The Realm of the Nebulae*. The idea of dark matter seemed to be gaining credibility.

Horace Babcock soon added more evidence. Observing the outer regions of the Andromeda galaxy, Babcock reported in 1939 that its outer region was spinning too quickly for its observed mass. In 1940, Jan Oort would report similar observations of another galaxy, further solidifying the narrative.

An Idea Ahead of Its Time

Still, the theory of dark matter did not gain mainstream acceptance among astronomers or astrophysicists or even the larger scientific community for quite some time. In 1959, Franz Kahn and Lo Woltjer began studying the movements of stars in what was called the Local Group, a group of several dozen galaxies, including the Milky Way and Andromeda. Their research showed that the Milky Way and Andromeda galaxies were moving in such a way that they must have a substantial bit of mass to them that remains unseen. Kahn and Woltjer suggested that invisible masses of hot gas might exist within the galaxies themselves or in the spaces between them.

By 1961, there was enough interest in this "missing matter" to prompt a special gathering during the International Astronomical Union's (IAU) General Assembly. The scientists who attended hoped to

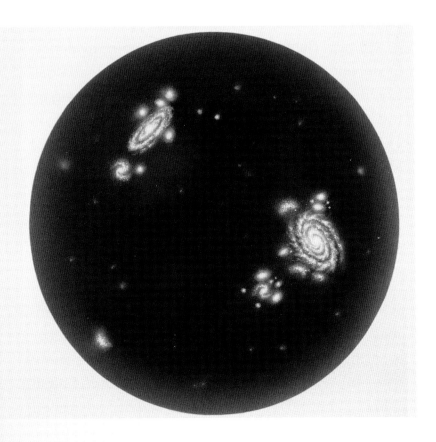

The Milky Way is one of a few dozen galaxies that make up the Local Group of galaxies, which is depicted here. The Local Group has a diameter of about three million light years.

develop concrete theories on galaxy clusters. They attempted to explain why they remained stable despite the evidence that they should fly apart. No consensus was reached. The mystery of dark matter would remain elusive.

Few had the patience or saw the urgency for a solution to the problem of the missing matter. In his book *The 4 Percent Universe*, Richard Panek explained, "In science, progress often follows a self-fulfilling logic: You work on the problems that have the best chance of yielding conclusions or are most in need of them." Because the motions of stars and galaxies were so poorly understood, there was little interest among most astronomers in pursuing these questions since the answers might be quite difficult to find.

While individual researchers and teams of researchers can often make incredible breakthroughs, the larger scientific community is more conservative and slow to fully accept new ideas. Many people must repeat and confirm the results of a theory over and over again before it is accepted as a scientific law. Better tools would also be needed to more accurately and efficiently measure the evidence that could put dark matter at the center of scientific research.

A NEW ERA IN DARK MATTER

Chapter 3

J ust as Galileo's use of the telescope proved revolutionary to seventeenth-century scientists studying space, twentieth-century scientists would benefit greatly from advances in technology. New tools would enable them to better observe the universe and measure the properties of galaxies. At the same time, scientists who went against old and accepted ways of thinking would use those new tools to make headway on the mystery of dark matter.

VERA RUBIN, PIONEER

Pioneering astronomer Vera Rubin began making waves in the 1950s with her observations of

Kitt Peak National Observatory, at an elevation of about 6,880 feet (2,096 meters), is located near Tucson, Arizona, and has the world's most diverse collection of astronomical instruments.

how galaxies behave. Aside from the importance of her research and discoveries, Rubin broke barriers as a female astronomer. Early on, in the July 15, 1954, issue of the *Proceedings of the National Academy of Sciences*, she published her doctoral thesis, "Fluctuations in the Space Distribution of the Galaxies." Her work centered on how galaxies seemed to arrange themselves in groups, or clusters. Even respected fellow scientists like Hubble had believed that this clustering was probably accidental or that the clusters they observed were optical illusions. Rubin thought differently. According to Richard Panek's *The 4 Percent Universe*, her conclusion was that "galaxies don't just bump and clump arbitrarily; they gather for a reason, and that reason is gravity." Rubin's research was largely ignored by the mainstream. However it gained notice in the astronomical community.

Her earlier work had been based on others' observations. However her later work was firsthand. In 1963, she started watching the stars from the Kitt Peak National Observatory near Tucson, Arizona. In 1964, she was the first woman to observe the heavens from Mt. Palomar Observatory, near San Diego, California. She also became the first female staff scientist at the Department of Terrestrial Magnetism (DTM), part of the Carnegie Institution for Science in Washington, D.C.

At that time, most astronomers studied the motion of nearby stars in the Milky Way. Rubin instead concentrated on more distant stars. First, she watched those on the outer edges of the Milky Way, and later she observed stars in other galaxies.

Rubin and Ford Team Up

One particular relationship would help Rubin make some new breakthroughs. At DTM, Rubin began working closely with astronomer W. Kent Ford. She had already studied motions of the Andromeda galaxy. She knew that most of the information she needed would not be obvious with the naked eye. Even powerful telescopes would not be helpful.

Ford had invented an advanced spectrograph, or spectrometer. Like Galileo's earlier break-throughs, and the ever more advanced telescopes since, Ford's tool advanced the technology of the time. Spectrometers measure light. They split light waves into different colors, which help determine the source material of the light. Previous spectrometers were extremely time consuming to use. Back in 1916, Francis G. Pease, an American astronomer, had needed as many as eighty-four hours over the course of three months to record, or expose, a spectrum of one tiny section of sky. This exposure time had been chopped down to about ten hours by the mid-1960s—still a time-consuming job. Ford's invention further cut this down by about 90 percent. It also helped prevent another problem, which was that combining different images of

the Andromeda from different nights sometimes caused errors in the calculations.

The Carnegie Image Tube Spectrograph was a sensitive instrument that could efficiently track the blue and red shifts of stars approaching and moving

Vera Rubin is shown measuring spectra at the Department of Terrestrial Magnetism in 1970. These measurements were integral to her dark matter revelations.

away, or receding, from an observer. Rubin and Ford observed these color shifts, called spectra, in different parts of Andromeda. Ford's faster equipment helped them obtain up to six measurements every night. They had also gone farther from Andromeda's center in their observations than anyone else had done for any galaxy previously. What they found was unusual.

SOME UNEXPECTED FINDINGS

For years, Newton's principles of gravitational force held science in its grasp. They had been applied to things ranging from the motions of the planets to those of larger bodies in the universe, like galaxies and galaxy clusters. The greater gravity of the sun makes the closer planets of the solar system, such as Mercury and Venus, revolve around the sun much more quickly than more distant ones, such as Jupiter, Saturn, or Neptune. Rubin and Ford expected the same rule to apply to stars in a galaxy. This meant that farther stars should revolve more slowly around the galaxy centers than the closer ones. They assumed that the galactic centers had way more mass, and hence greater gravitational fields, than their outer reaches. No one had observed otherwise because, before Ford's spectrograph, they had simply been unable to.

Rubin and Ford actually found that the stars they observed, as well as the gas and other matter of the outer reaches of Andromeda, revolved around the galaxy's center at the same rate as the stars and gas closest to it. While they had doubts about the reason behind this discovery, they submitted their research in 1969 to the *Astrophysical Journal*. The difference in levels of rotation velocities, or speeds, was mapped on a chart. Usually, scientists presenting data in this way would show a "rotation curve." But there was no curve in Rubin and Ford's data. Instead, it remained pretty much flat.

This exciting observation raised more questions than it answered. Why did the outer stars behave the same as the inner ones? Did extra gravitational force exist where others had not earlier detected it? The distribution of matter in a spiral galaxy had always been assumed to concentrate in its center, or core,

area. According to the book *Cosmic Horizons*, Vera
Rubin put it simply when she said, "What you see in
a spiral galaxy…is not what you get."

A Hidden Universe, Revealed

Thinking over a solution to this new puzzle, Vera Rubin
remembered reading about a similar phenomenon
during her days as a graduate student in physics.
She was remembering Fritz Zwicky's thoughts on
dark matter. An excited Rubin realized that she,
with Ford's help, may have documented evidence of
Zwicky's original idea: that there is far more matter in
a galaxy than what is visible. She realized this could
explain the flat rotation curves of the near and distant parts of Andromeda.

Rubin and Ford's Andromeda observations
seemed to back up Zwicky's original ideas. Since
the farther stars were moving more rapidly than
expected, the visible mass of the center of the galaxy
was not enough to keep these outer stars in orbit.
According to the accepted rules, they should fly out
of their orbits, out into space. Where there is more
matter, there should be greater gravity affecting its
relationship to other matter. A great deal of "hidden" or dark matter might explain why outer stars

revolved around galactic centers as fast as the closer ones. Similar to Zwicky's own findings, Rubin calculated that some galaxies had as much as ten times more invisible matter than visible matter.

They repeated their experiments with dozens of other spiral galaxies and got the same results. In 1974, they combined the use of Ford's spectrograph with a new 13-foot (4-meter) telescope at Kitt Peak Observatory. Using these, they looked even farther into the universe and along the arms of spiral galaxies. By 1978, they had published the results of their research, showing that the rotation curves for eight other galaxies were the same: all flat.

THE OUTER HALOS: NESTS OF DARK MATTER?

Another assumption about the visible mass in galaxies was challenged by this theory about unseen matter. Rubin suspected that while the visible stars make it appear that a galaxy's mass concentrates in the center, it was possible that more of their mass may lie in the galaxy's outer reaches. The whole mass of dark matter forms a halo around the luminous parts. She even theorized that large patches of space between galaxies could be filled with dark matter, too.

This view of the galaxy NGC 4555 was revealed by NASA's Chandra X-ray Observatory. Scientists believed dark matter might provide the gravitational force that binds its gas cloud to its core of stars.

Many members of the astronomical and larger scientific communities had their doubts about the basic existence of dark matter to begin with. Zwicky had faced such doubts himself in the 1930s, partly due to his reputation. Many others had doubted Rubin because she was a woman. But Rubin and Ford's repeated observations and simple explanation could

GAINING ACCEPTANCE

Rubin's discoveries meant that one of two likely explanations was true. The first was that the standard explanations of gravity and galactic motion were somehow wrong. The other was they were right, but that dark matter had to exist, too. For many scientists, rethinking some of the most established laws of astrophysics was difficult, even unthinkable. Others were stubborn and at first resisted the proof of dark matter, but they were likely even more stubborn about abandoning the theory of gravity in favor of new explanations. While scientists must always be ready to accept new facts as evidence grows, they can also be slow to change their minds. Theories developed by Isaac Newton and Albert Einstein had to survive many challenges over the centuries and decades, respectively.

not be denied. Sandra Faber and Jay Gallagher, writing in the *Annual Review of Astronomy and Astrophysics* in 1979, declared that "the case for invisible mass in the universe is very strong and getting stronger."

Finally, the idea that all matter in the universe had to produce or reflect light was questioned. Talking about this assumption, and how much they had taken it for granted in their early work, Rubin often said, according to Panek's *The 4 Percent Universe*, "Nobody ever told us that all matter radiated. We just assumed that it did." Rubin and Ford's research once again showed that scientists must never make blanket assumptions and that everything can and should be questioned. With their work, they had ushered in a new era for scientists' understanding of the universe.

The Ancient History of Dark Matter

Around the same time that Rubin's work was becoming accepted by the scientific community, another mysterious substance was being investigated. This substance was almost as old as the big bang, but no one had yet been able to detect it.

Arno Penzias and Robert Wilson of Bell Labs accidentally discovered the cosmic microwave background (CMB) radiation in 1965 using a large cosmic antenna in Holmdel, New Jersey. The two scientists were trying to analyze distant radio waves from the fringe of the Milky Way. However, they could not account for a background signal noise bouncing off the antenna. They soon realized it was something that many scientists had predicted would be possible to detect but had never done so.

The CMB was leftover radiation from about 380,000 years after the big bang, from when the

Arno Penzias *(left)* and Robert
W. Wilson stand in front of their
microwave radio antenna at the
Bell Labs Holmdel Complex in
New Jersey on October 18, 1978.

universe had cooled down from its early extreme heat. It seemed to fill the universe and could be detected at a very low temperature, 2.7 Kelvin, or -454.81° F. This was only a few degrees higher than the coldest temperature possible, called absolute zero (-459.67° F, or 273.15° C).

Later, when scientists were able to use very precise tools to measure CMB throughout space, they mapped very tiny differences, or fluctuations, from 2.7 Kelvin. These were called anisotropies. The fluctuations were as small as 0.00001 higher or lower than 2.7 K. The resulting picture they gained from these observations showed that there were differences in how matter had organized itself when it first formed. Based on these slight differences in heat, scientists could tell that dark matter behaved differently than the baryonic matter that formed to make "normal" matter. At 380,000 years old, scientists believe that the universe had about five times as much dark matter as normal matter.

WHAT DARK MATTER ISN'T

Chapter

4

Scientists have only indirect proof, however strong, of dark matter's existence. They also have little idea of what it actually is. Rubin and Ford helped revive interest in dark matter. From the 1980s on, scientists continued to examine the theory. They knew dark matter did not emit or reflect light, or it would have been visible. They believed strongly that it was matter of some kind. They also guessed that it had mass that exerted gravitational force. But what was it, really? For years, scientists have been split on the nature of this mysterious stuff.

Some researchers defined dark matter as anything that did not give off electromagnetic radiation of any kind—no infrared or ultraviolet radiation, radio waves, X-rays, or gamma rays. In this sense, "It is truly 'dark,'" as Rhett Herman and Shane L. Marson told *Scientific American* in 1998. Scientists have noted that dark matter probably surrounds galaxies in large, spherical formations known as galactic halos. These are the outer sections of galaxies that have fewer stars.

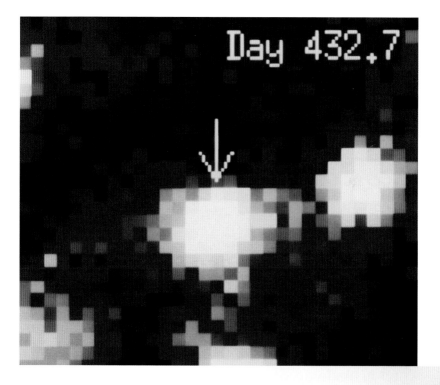

A brown dwarf star in the halo of the Milky Way galaxy is depicted in a possible gravitational lensing event taking place in the Large Magellanic Cloud (LMC).

Some scientists believed that dark matter may actually have been comprised of objects they had already discovered but that emitted little or almost no light at all. When they are found in the halos of galaxies, they are called massive astrophysical compact halo objects, or MACHOs. When MACHOs were discovered in 1993, some believed that they were the important missing piece of the dark matter puzzle. Others thought that the solution to dark matter meant looking more closely at tiny and even subatomic particles that had been theorized even earlier, called WIMPs. MACHOs suggested a dark matter solution based on baryonic, or "normal" matter, and were considered a more conservative or traditional solution. WIMPs, which are weakly interacting massive particles, were thought to be entirely new and undiscovered, and they were considered more of a radical answer.

PUTTING MACHOS TO THE TEST

Scientists who favor the theory that MACHOs make up dark matter have tended to believe that dark matter is made up of "normal" baryonic matter. Several space phenomena that qualified were thought to be good candidates for what dark matter might be and were classified as MACHOs. They ranged in size from low-mass stars and included white dwarfs, neutron stars, and even supermassive black holes.

Low-mass stars were a possible candidate because stars with a much lower mass than, say, Earth's sun, might burn much less of their fuel and thus emit much less light. Ones that are small and dark enough might be candidates for dark matter.

As authors David and Richard Garfinkle state in their book *Three Steps to the Universe*, "We know that stars do not burn fuel forever, and that eventually each star becomes one of three kinds of 'dead

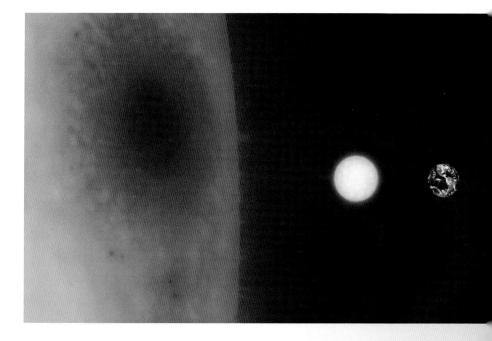

This artist's representation helps show the relative size of a white dwarf star *(center)* compared to the sun *(left)* and Earth. White dwarfs are far denser than Earth, however.

stars'—white dwarf, neutron star, or black hole." Researchers believed former stars might account for dark matter. This assumed that there were far more dead stars than live ones in the universe.

GRAVITATIONAL LENSING: SEEING THE INVISIBLE

One innovative technique allowed astronomers to detect and count certain types of objects in galaxy halos, even ones invisible to the naked eye. This is called gravitational lensing. Just like many of the techniques used in the search for dark matter, it is a way of working around the problem of looking for something we cannot see.

Just as ordinary lenses made of glass bend light, other objects bend light, too. Gravity affects physical matter. This is why a ball thrown in the air comes back down. Gravity also affects light radiation traveling through the universe. Some amount of light will be drawn by an object's gravitational field and bend around the object, its path slightly changed.

Gravitational lensing is a way to prove that something unseen actually exists between the light source and the observer. Just as important, it shows that the object has some kind of gravitational field. That indicates it has mass.

Lensing can detect MACHOs such as a brown dwarf or a black hole, as well as other objects. MACHOs focus light rays, making it appear that the light source behind it is brightening. Even before the technology was advanced enough to prove it, Albert Einstein predicted in 1919 that gravity would bend light rays and could turn celestial objects into such lenses. Lensing has also been refined to estimate the mass and size of possible MACHOs, based on distance and the duration of a lensing effect.

BLACK HOLES

Black holes are extremely massive concentrations of matter. They contain so much matter in such a small space that their gravitational fields suck in everything around them. Some of these are stars that have burned out and "collapsed" upon themselves. Stars and other objects in space rotate around black holes, but only from a safe distance. The gravitational pull of a black hole can be so powerful that even nearby light is absorbed. This is why black holes remain invisible to the naked eye.

Black holes can be extremely tiny, as small as an atom. But an atom-sized black hole could have the mass of an entire mountain. Others are "stellar" black holes, so-called because they are often larger than Earth's sun, some as much as twenty times bigger. The largest ones are called supermassive black holes. Scientists have credible proof that there may be gigantic black holes in the centers of galaxies. The Milky Way, for example, is believed by many to revolve around the supermassive black hole Sagittarius A. Its mass is approximately the same as four million stars.

For a time, scientists thought that black holes might qualify as MACHOs. Then they would solve the mystery of dark matter. The way black holes were first detected was similar to the early research that sparked the dark matter debate. Like dark matter, they were invisible to normal telescopes. This made it necessary to find second-hand evidence of their existence. This evidence included the gravitational effects black holes had on the objects around them. Finding stars circling around something that remains invisible is a way for astronomers to locate the presence of a black hole.

Brown Dwarfs and Red Dwarfs

Like Earth's sun, brown dwarfs are made of the element hydrogen. Unlike the sun and other stars, they

Red dwarfs are among the smallest stars in the universe.
The one shown here is a flare star, a subset of red dwarfs
that flare up every three to four hours.

are much smaller. They also do not have enough gravity to ignite. The nuclear reactions that create light and heat like those that occur in our sun do not happen in brown dwarfs. They are simply big masses of hydrogen gas held together by their own gravity. They emit a bit of heat and little light compared to other stars. They proved enough of a mystery to earlier researchers that some scientists became excited by them. They thought these stars might be the answer to the dark matter mystery.

Other low-mass celestial objects have also been proposed as a solution to dark matter. Red dwarfs are any low-mass stars less than half the mass of our sun. By comparison to the sun, they also produce very little light. They make about 1/10,000th of the energy it does. Researchers in the 1990s had hoped to discover many red dwarfs, which could then account for dark matter. Rubin and Ford had started a trend in dark matter research. These low-mass stars were the most popular answer to the question of what dark matter is among many astronomers and astrophysicists.

In 1994, John Bahcall and Andrew Gould surveyed much of the Milky Way's halo, expecting to find many red dwarfs. Around the same time, the powerful Hubble Space Telescope helped Francesco Paresce search for brown dwarfs and red dwarfs in the halos of the Milky Way and nearby galaxies. The images Hubble produced, however, backed up

Bahcall and Gould's findings: there were far fewer red dwarfs than expected. According to a November 1994 article in the *Christian Science Monitor*, Bahcall said, "The universe is such that less than 16 percent of dark matter is made of faint stars."

One of the most prominent researchers of brown dwarfs also admitted in 2003 that brown dwarfs will probably make up only part of the puzzle. Astronomy professor Ian S. McLean told *UCLA News* in September 2003 that brown dwarfs are very numerous in the universe, and they "could make a small, but significant contribution to dark matter." He added, "Brown dwarfs won't account for all of the so-called dark matter. The rest is presumably a new form of matter."

THE VERDICT ON MACHOS

Several astronomical teams searched for evidence of MACHOs in the late twentieth century. The MACHO project, along with the EROS and OGLE projects, all monitored stars in galaxies neighboring ours, including the Small Magellanic Cloud (SMC), the Large Magellanic Cloud (LMC), and the Galactic Bulge. They used gravitational microlensing to watch these galaxies for several years. In 1993, the MACHO and

EROS teams reported that they had detected three
MACHOs. By then, the MACHO team had examined
1.8 million stars for a year and EROS had observed 3
million for three years. By the end of the 1990s, the
three teams had reported about twenty microlensing
events. The search for dark matter was proving to be
difficult and intensive.

In recent years, many astronomers have acknowl-
edged that low-mass stars and MACHOs in general

Particle physicist Evalyn Gates is shown here in a
promotional photo at the Cleveland Museum of
Natural History, Ohio, taken when Gates became
director of the institution.

probably do not make up much of the mysterious matter that we cannot see out in space. Evalyn Gates, writing in her 2009 book, *Einstein's Telescope: The Hunt for Dark Matter and Dark Energy in the Universe*, wrote that "MACHOs, the least exotic candidates for dark matter, have now been effectively ruled out as the main component of the dark matter." They remain fascinating subjects of study, but the search continues, with some scientists still counting on MACHOs, while others are looking elsewhere.

The MACHO team's final results, revealed in 2000, concluded that MACHOs did not make up more than 20 percent of the galactic halos they had observed. EROS team members also reported low percentages of MACHOs.

Dark Matter's Implications

Rubin realized that the idea of dark matter had affected the debate among astronomers and astrophysicists about the fate of the universe itself. Once, scientists had argued between two models of the universe. There was the steady state, in which the universe remained basically unchanging. The other was the big bang theory, in which the universe was constantly changing and expanding.

A SUPER-SIZED UNIVERSE?

Yale University's Pieter van Dokkum said in 2010 that his team's study of nearby galaxies revealed far more red dwarfs than expected. While the Milky Way seemed to have few, Van Dokkum's target galaxies had three times as many stars as originally believed. These included twenty times more red dwarfs in these galaxies than in our own.

Three planets orbit a young red dwarf star in this artist's conception. Red dwarfs are dimmer and smaller than yellow stars, like Earth's sun.

These were far greater numbers than Bahcall and Gould had detected in their earlier studies of other adjacent galaxies.

Van Dokkum's fellow participant in the project, Charlie Conroy, added, "We usually assume other galaxies look like our own. But this suggests other conditions are possible in other galaxies." Even if red dwarfs are not dark matter, per se, they might be part of the puzzle. A bigger universe, with more red dwarfs than expected, gave those who dismissed the theory of MACHOs something to think about.

How would dark matter, if such a thing really exists, affect the size, character, and behavior of the universe within five, ten, or fifteen billion years? Richard Panek, in *The 4 Percent Universe*, repeated a quote of Rubin's from *Science* magazine in which she said that learning dark matter's secrets would help answer these questions. "Not until we learn the characteristics and spatial distribution of dark matter... can we predict whether the universe is of high density, so that the expansion will ultimately be halted and the universe will start to contract, or of low density, and so that the expansion will go on forever."

Panek's options for how the story of the universe will play out are part of a threefold path that many scientists are currently debating, or predicting: closed, open, and flat. If the universe is closed, some astronomers argue, gravity will eventually pull the universe back into the single point. Lemaître's "primeval atom" will be reborn. Some call this the big crunch. A gigantic black hole made up of all the matter in the known universe will form.

Others predict an open universe, in which all the galaxies, stars, and all matter in general, will continue expanding forever. A flat universe is another scenario, in which gravity eventually stops universal expansion, but the universe does not reverse and begin to contract.

Discovering how dark matter works, and more important, what it is, will give scientists a better idea of how much gravity may eventually affect the universe. With a great deal of dark matter, many scientists predict a closed universe. Less might mean a flat universe.

As some scientists developed theories about MACHOs, others looked inward and into the very nature of matter itself. They sought the secrets to dark matter not in distant space, but much, much closer.

THE SEARCH FOR DARK MATTER

Chapter

5

Unlike astronomers and astrophysicists looking for MACHOs in the sky, particle physicists
look for dark matter at the tiny, subatomic
level. Particle physicists are trying to prove the existence of another candidate for dark matter. They are
called WIMPs.

Weakly interacting massive particles, or WIMPs,
are so named because they tend not to interact with
other matter. Their only interaction may be gravitational. Unlike MACHOs, which are made of the
normal stuff of the universe, WIMPs are believed to
pass through ordinary matter and to be nonbaryonic
in nature.

Technicians work on a WIMP detector at the UK Dark Matter Collaboration (UKDMC), located at Boulby Mine in England. About 3,609 feet (1,110 m) of rock prevent cosmic rays from affecting the detector.

The problem with MACHOs has been that they cannot be seen because they are too dark and too far away. The problem with WIMPs is that the particles and objects that they might consist of are too small to see. When they come into contact with baryonic matter, they may not behave the same as other baryonic matter.

Like your arm passing through air, WIMPs might pass through your body and you would not even feel them. Scientists believe that certain WIMPs might be as tiny as five hundred thousand times smaller than an electron, while others believe that even smaller ones exist. These are particles far too tiny to see with one's eyes or even detect with a microscope. Still, many efforts are mounted worldwide at this very moment, hoping to be the first to "discover" dark matter.

Investigating WIMPs

Catching a WIMP interaction with normal matter may be many times more complicated than searching for a needle in a haystack. If they indeed exist, millions of WIMPs, even trillions of them, may pass through each human being every few seconds. Another estimate shows that about one hundred thousand WIMPs could pass through every square centimeter of Earth's mass per second. Their numbers would have to be very great to account for the "missing mass" of dark matter.

Neutrinos are particles first conceived of in the 1930s. They were finally discovered in the 1950s. These incredibly tiny particles travel at almost the speed of light and barely interact with matter. Some scientists initially thought neutrinos could be dark matter. However, much of the research on WIMPs has determined that dark matter particles will likely move slower and be much larger than neutrinos.

Neutralinos might also be dark matter. These particles are yet to be discovered. They are thought to be like neutrinos, only slower and heavier. The theory of their existence predates the search for WIMPs as dark matter.

HUNTING WIMPs: DIRECT DETECTION

The search for dark matter takes scientists to some pretty cold places and demands some extreme measures. It has also required many teams to spend a great deal of money to create sites where theories about WIMPs could be tested properly. A number of research teams have aimed to create very specific conditions in which they hope to cause and observe some interaction between ordinary matter and WIMPs. While these experiments cannot force interactions, the scientists hope at least to make them more possible.

A major problem is the technology needed to set up and observe these experiments. The instruments involved must be able to see reactions that are happening on a level even smaller than subatomic. These reactions can include tiny bits of light or heat or a measurement of electrons being knocked off in part of the detector.

According to Iain Nicholson's *Dark Side of the Universe*, another big problem is that scientists must eliminate things that could prevent these reactions from happening. They also have to make sure nothing prevents them from seeing the very delicate and tiny changes they are looking for. "For every possible WIMP interaction, there are millions of unwanted background events." These can include cosmic rays from outer space, or temperatures that could sabotage the experiment. "The materials used to construct WIMP detectors," Nicholson points out, "have to be very carefully selected and purified to reduce radioactive impurities to an absolute minimum."

Many current experiments are therefore being done in underground environments that are well protected. At the same time, no experiment can get rid of every possible background event. Even the very low radiation in underground rocks found in certain WIMP experiment locations can foul up a research team's results.

CRYOGENIC DARK MATTER SEARCH (CDMS)

In the late 1980s, Bernard Sadoulet and Walter Stockwell of the Center for Particle Astrophysics set in motion the Cryogenic Dark Matter Search (CDMS). It was an experiment that aimed to detect WIMPs using an underground tunnel. What the scientists hoped to create and document was a collision between the nucleus of a regular atom and a WIMP.

The CDMS was originally housed in a shallow tunnel under the campus of Stanford University in Palo Alto, California. Because the background and particle radiation in the area was high, in 2003 the scientists had CDMS II built in the Soudan Mine in Minnesota.

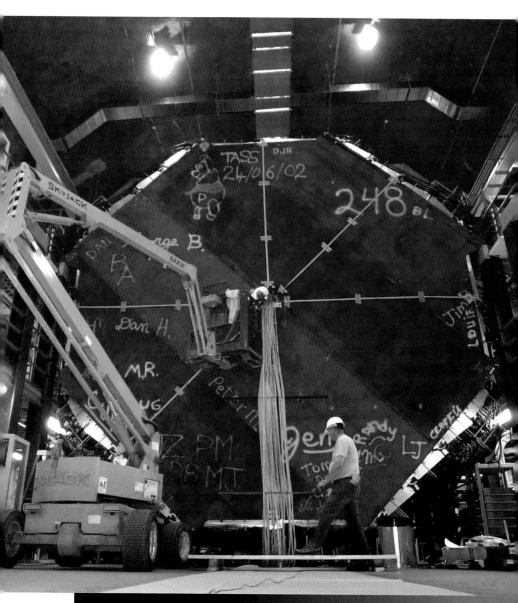

Workers are shown completing a physics lab located at the Soudan Mine near Soudan, Minnesota. Underground sites provide optimal conditions for dark matter research.

This time, they buried the experiment more than a mile down—2,559 feet (780 m).

"Cryogenic" referred to the extremely cold conditions that were necessary for the experiment to potentially work. The detectors used in CDMS were made of the elements germanium or silicon. They were cooled to only a degree or so above absolute zero. This is a temperature at which there is almost no molecular motion whatsoever. A disruption of a nucleus from a WIMP at this temperature was theoretically easier to detect.

SMALL VICTORIES

Like many of the other WIMP-hunting experiments, CDMS has not yet detected concrete proof. However, scientists from CDMS and other experiments have reported, using estimates of how big they expect WIMPs to be, that their tools and techniques improved their detection abilities a few times over since the hunt for WIMPs began. Richard Panek's *The 4 Percent Universe* related how the members of the CDMS team had gathered in 2008 to find out how many stray or unwanted "hits" from non-WIMPs they had accidentally registered. The fewer they registered, the smaller an area of phase space they would have to search in the future. When they learned it was zero, they cheered.

Even success, when it happened for the CDMS team, posed more questions than it answered. Two detections were recorded in August and October 2007, on two different detectors. Jodi Cooley, the team's data analyst, ran numerous quality checks to make sure the data were solid.

When they announced their results, a buzz went up in the scientific community, especially in the science blogosphere. Many people prematurely reported that they had "discovered dark matter." Eventually, they announced their two detections, but they could not say one way or the other what these meant. Cooley eventually explained: "The results of this experiment cannot be interpreted as significant evidence for WIMP interactions, but we cannot reject either event as a signal." It seemed that even when dark matter researchers did not lose, they did not quite win, either.

SECOND-GENERATION DETECTORS

Other WIMP-hunting researchers influenced by CDMS hurried to launch their own detection experiments. Newer facilities made use of noble gases (argon, neon, and xenon). These gases did not need to be cooled nearly as much to detect WIMPs. They were far cheaper, too.

XENON100 was set up in Gran Sasso, Italy, in 2006. It used a 33.06-pound (15 kilogram) tank of xenon as the material they hoped would "catch" a WIMP. By 2007, while it had failed to detect WIMP signatures, the lab had gotten a reputation for having among the most sensitive and effective instruments for potentially catching WIMP detections. Scientists had also claimed they narrowed the search for them substantially. The same team has set up newer versions of the project, using ever-greater amounts of xenon.

An American team recently began an even more advanced search using xenon. The Large Underground Xenon (LUX) experiment, like ones before it, is looking for signs of the faint interaction between ordinary matter and WIMP dark matter.

INDIRECT DETECTION: THE AMANDA PROJECT

The Antarctica Muon and Neutrino Detector Array, or AMANDA project, was one of several important efforts in the last two decades to detect tiny particles that may prove to originate from the interactions between dark matter particles or between dark matter

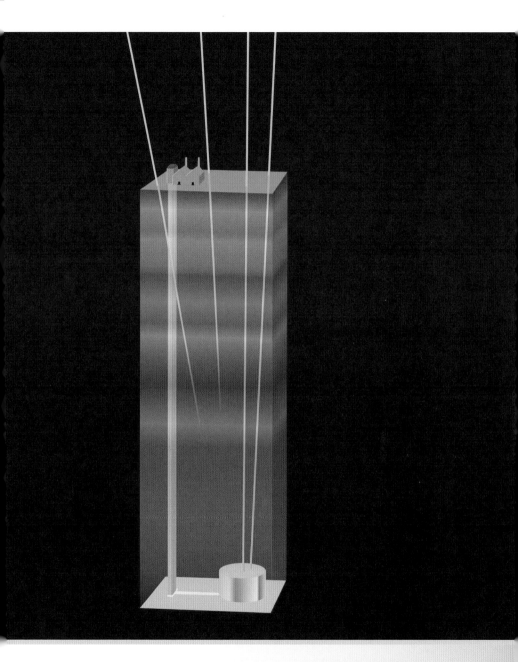

This artist's conception of England's Boulby Mine shows cosmic rays *(in blue)* being blocked by the deep rock, while the yellow lines show the theoretical WIMPs the scientists hope to detect.

and normal particles. AMANDA was a neutrino tele-scope built at the South Pole by an international team of scientists. Neutrinos are not deflected in their travels because they pass through almost every other kind of matter. They originate from high-energy events and places, like supernovas or black holes, and even from within Earth's hot, molten core. Because they travel in straight lines, they can potentially tell scientists about where they originate.

In this case, a possible byproduct of WIMPs was thought to hold the key to detecting them. The powerful nuclear reactions of the sun are thought to create conditions that make WIMPs annihilate, or destroy, each other. These interactions produce high-energy neutrinos, which travel through space. The AMANDA telescope was actually not a traditional telescope. It included many orbs—spherical particle detectors—frozen in ice up to a mile down. These could detect the neutrinos penetrating through hundreds of meters of that ice. The ice therefore served as part of a massive WIMP detector. Neutrinos were noted that came from Earth's atmosphere, but none were proven to have come from the sun, unfortunately.

AMANDA and other projects fall under the category of indirect detection experiments. These attempt to show the presence of WIMPs by using proof of second-hand phenomena that WIMPs may influence. Other such experiments include gamma-ray

CAN WE MAKE DARK MATTER?

The Large Hadron Collider (LHC) in Geneva, Switzerland, is a circular, 17-mile-long (27 km) tunnel that serves as a particle collider, the world's largest. It speeds up particles of matter to 99.9999991 percent the speed of light and smashes them together. The collider was built to try and create, and then study, theoretical particles that scientists could not find in nature. Its greatest success was the forty-year search for the Higgs boson particle in 2012. Its discovery supported the Standard Model of particle physics. Particle physicists also developed a theory called supersymmetry to account for the bizarre behaviors of high-energy particles. Because this new theory imagines particles that behave much like dark matter is predicted to behave, dark matter researchers hope that experiments using the LHC may even help create artificial WIMPs for study. So far, however, scientists' failure to find any of the particles to support this theory may force researchers to look elsewhere.

detectors because WIMPs are also theorized to decay and produce gamma-ray photons, or light particles. Experiments include the Cherenkov Telescope Array (CTA), a series of telescopes covering both the northern and southern hemispheres of Earth's surface that can register gamma rays. There is also the Fermi Gamma-Ray Space Telescope (FGST), which was launched into a low Earth orbit in 2008 by the National Aeronautics and Space Administration (NASA).

OUTER-SPACE DARK MATTER LABS

Tools in the search for dark matter have reached into outer space itself. Nobel Prize–winning physicist Samuel Ting fought for years to get the $1.5 billion, 18,500-pound (8,391.5 kg) Alpha Magnetic Spectrometer (AMS) installed in low Earth orbit. It has been 200 miles (322 km) up, on the International Space Station (ISS), since May 2011.

The AMS was designed for two missions: to detect and measure antimatter in cosmic rays and to detect evidence of dark matter. The spectrometer looked for positrons, which are the antimatter counterparts to electrons. Positrons are destroyed when they touch ordinary matter, so they are largely undetectable on Earth's surface or in underground labs, but they can be detected in the vacuum of space. The theory behind AMS also assumed that WIMPs colliding in distant space would annihilate each other and create gamma rays and positrons.

The Alpha Magnetic Spectrometer (AMS) is shown
here parked on the International Space Station (ISS).
AMS represented the largest scientific collaboration
to use the station and was funded by sixteen different
nations.

So far, AMS has collected only 8 percent of the
expected data it will observe through the year 2028,
and it has not reported any conclusive results yet. But
Ting told a conference in 2013 that the spectrometer
had observed more than four hundred thousand positrons. These were detected as coming from many
different directions. For Ting, this confirmed that
they could very well be the result of WIMP collisions
in deep space, rather than the results of a single and

faraway cosmic event, which would likely all come from the same direction.

AMS is one of several space-based dark matter investigative projects. Others include the Wilkinson Microwave Anisotropy Probe (WMAP). This NASA mission, launched in 2001, helped map the CMB (cosmic microwave background). It proved to many scientists the important role of dark matter in the history of the universe, among many other accomplishments. Richard Panek, in *The 4 Percent Universe*, described WMAP's greatest success as a "baby picture of the universe…the matter-and-energy equivalent of the universe's DNA." Another lab is the Planck space observatory, launched in 2009 by the European Space Agency (ESA). Planck provided scientists with more data about the possible percentages of dark matter in the universe and provided even more exact maps of the CMB.

THE PROBLEM WITH DARK MATTER

Chapter

6

The competition to be the first to discover evidence of dark matter—especially WIMPs—has grown fierce in the last decade. So little evidence has been found that when it is reported, a research team's peers and competitors demand further proof. Tensions can even arise between groups of researchers when they disagree on findings.

At the same time, some researchers believe there are other places to search for dark matter or that different search methods should be applied. Still others believe that after such a long search, it might be time to consider other theories. Perhaps the long-accepted laws of gravitation of Newton and Einstein must be updated, rather than relied on, to insist on the elusive presence of dark matter.

THE DAMA CONTROVERSY

Alongside their neighbors at the XENON100 experiment, another team had been conducting a WIMP-finding mission at Gran Sasso National Laboratory in Italy. The Italian-led project, DAMA (short for DArk MAtter), had used 551 pounds (250 kg) of crystalline sodium iodide as the catching material for WIMPs. During its twelve years of operation as of 2011, the researchers reported they had recorded seasonal fluctuations of hits. They claimed these were the result of dark matter particles. The hits matched the predicted, theoretical results of the passage of Earth through a sea of WIMPs during the solar system's rotations in the universe, they said.

Many other dark matter researchers questioned the results. Mario Livio, of the Space Telescope Science Institute, told *Scientific American*, "I think everyone would agree at this point that they see a signal. The question is: What is it?" This is a natural question for any scientific team. Others have claimed that the DAMA team has not been as open as it

This is the Oscillation Project with Emulsion-Racking Apparatus (OPERA) detector's bricks, which were designed to detect neutrinos.

should be in releasing its raw data for other scientists to analyze and confirm its results.

Conflicting results from the XENON100 project next door caused even more debate among the dark matter community. In May 2011, several research teams presented results at a dark matter symposium at the Space Telescope Science Institute. Both DAMA and XENON100 presented as well. Both teams' experiments work in a similar fashion. However, XENON100 had an even better reputation for its ultrasensitive detection equipment, which had eliminated more background noise than any other project seeking direct evidence of WIMPs. The XENON100 team had not detected any dark matter signals, much less any seasonal fluctuations. On the surface, it seemed that their results were completely incompatible.

One of the DAMA team's leaders, Pierluigi Belli, countered that his team had eliminated many alternative explanations for their readings. "It is quite difficult to demonstrate that it's not dark matter," he told *Scientific American.* "We cannot explain it in another way."

A third research team presenting at the symposium seemed to split the difference between DAMA and XENON100's results. Juan Collar, of the Coherent Germanium Neutrino Technology (CoGeNT) team, said that his project, before suffering a fire that delayed its research, had begun to see results similar to those of DAMA. However, CoGeNT members supported DAMA cautiously. "We're not going to claim we're seeing WIMPs," Collar said. At the same time, Collar pointed out that XENON100's detector might be the wrong equipment. It might not be able to observe the kind

THE MYSTERY OF DARK ENERGY

Perhaps even more mysterious than dark matter is the theory of dark energy. Most scientists now agree that less than 5 percent of the universe is normal matter. In recent years, their opinions have changed about what the remainder is. Dark matter was supposed to account for all the rest—that is, until dark energy was conceived of. Scientists believe that dark energy is either a property of space or its own form of energy that is helping to expand the universe. Whatever it may turn out to be, it estimated that the universe is about 5 percent normal matter, 25 percent dark matter, and 70 percent dark energy.

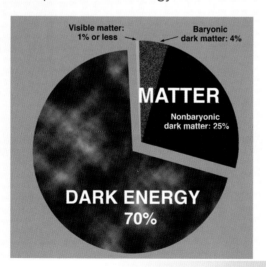

This diagram shows how visible matter may account for as little as 1 percent of the universe, while dark energy may account for around 70 percent.

of light WIMPs DAMA had claimed it had detected. Later data collected by the CoGeNT team up until April 2013 showed that they continued to find particle interactions that might be WIMPs.

Dark Matter's Skeptics

Because of so many inconclusive experiments, other scientists are beginning to question whether dark matter really exists. Others have been skeptical for some time. They believe that some other explanations should be considered. Others believe special exceptions should be made to Newton's and Einstein's laws of physics. These exceptions would better explain phenomena that were theorized to be caused by dark matter. The flat galactic rotation curves that Vera Rubin noted would be one.

Others believe that a combination of different types of matter will add up to the large amount of "missing matter" out there.

Astrophysicist Mario Livio and astronomer Joe Silk argued that "dark matter may not comprise one type of particle—as many current searches assume—but many." If this is true, then too many experiments looking for the same thing may be a waste of resources that could better be spent elsewhere.

Pictured here are three of the four optical telescopes that make up the European Southern Observatory (ESO) in Paranal, Chile. They are considered to be the world's most advanced optical instruments.

True dark matter skeptics believe that alternate theories may provide a more accurate explanation of how
the universe works. At the very least, researchers presenting alternative theories will keep the field of dark
matter research honest. One of the more interesting
challenges to dark matter came early on, as the field
was just getting off the ground in the late 1970s and
early 1980s.

Israeli physicist Mordehai Milgrom proposed
in 1983 that there was another explanation for
why the stars and galaxies behaved the way they
did. He theorized that it had little to do with extra
unseen matter in the universe. Milgrom thought
Rubin's flat rotation curves and the galactic motions
recorded by Zwicky and later scientists could be
better explained by rethinking Newtonian physics.
Scientists apply Newtonian physics throughout the
universe. Milgrom wondered, why not try out the
theory that certain objects moved differently on
a galactic scale? His theory assumed a change in
certain calculations of how gravity worked for very
small accelerations. He called this idea Modified
Newtonian Dynamics, or MOND.

Because Newtonian physics is considered almost
sacred to many scientists, MOND caused great

controversy at the time. In fact, it continues to do so. Still, a few scientists admit that MOND may do a better job of explaining motion, at least on the scale of galaxies. MOND's supporters claim that the search for dark matter may have gotten out of hand. They say that researchers can invent any kind of qualities they want for dark matter and that it can be distributed any way in the universe that scientists desire. Some hardcore skeptics believe that dark matter was invented by scientists to fix the contradictions between Newtonian laws and the evidence seen in galactic motions.

University of Maryland professor and astronomer Stacy McGaugh has questioned whether dark matter really exists, too. He was surprised to find that some of Milgrom's MOND principles worked with his own theories on Low Surface Brightness Galaxies. Using MOND-based formulas, he found their predictions closely matched the observations he made of forty-seven different galaxies and the relationships between their visible mass and rotational speeds.

In an interview with *Vice* magazine, McGaugh explained that one of his problems with dark matter research is its inconclusiveness. "If you run direct detection experiments for five years and don't find anything [...] you can go back to your models and tweak things until the dark matter particle is harder to find. You might be able to prove it's not neutralinos, for example. But that doesn't preclude you from coming up with something harder to detect." This process can theoretically go on forever, McGaugh says.

MOND's many critics, including most of the astrophysical scientific community, say that the MOND theories poorly explain other phenomena, such as how the universe has expanded, cosmic microwave

CHINA ENTERS THE RACE FOR DARK MATTER

Buried 8,200 feet (2,500 m) beneath Earth's surface in China's Sichuan province is the newest competitor in the race for dark matter, dubbed the PandaX project. Starting with 265 pounds (120 kg) of xenon, the Chinese project team hopes to ramp up to 2,205 pounds (1,000 kg) by 2016. The size of the project is ambitious and shows the seriousness of China's scientific community in finding the WIMPs that other teams have yet to find conclusively. They also hope to challenge and surpass the sensitivity of the equipment of the XENON100 project. PandaX has a definite advantage. Being so deep in the earth means that the project will have less exposure to outside cosmic rays than all the others.

background (CMB) radiation, and galaxies clustering since the big bang. MOND's supporters believe that it is worthwhile to challenge any belief system, even if MOND does not turn out to be completely right or wrong. Much like Zwicky doing his research in the 1930s, challenges to dark matter theories may remain unpopular now. But few can tell where new research may lead us in five, ten, or fifty years from now.

A glass lathe is used to make a dark matter scintillation (light) detector. Scientific instruments have to be especially precise and sophisticated to measure the tiny particles involved in this research.

A CROWDED FIELD

Dark matter research may also become a victim of its own success. There are four major ongoing xenon-based experiments looking for dark matter WIMPs worldwide, and many other researchers are working on indirect detection. Some scientists have pointed out that competing projects might be a waste of limited resources.

Such competition has been motivated by nationalist competition, at least partly. China originally asked the United States Department of Energy (DOE) to partner with it on PandaX. The DOE declined the invitation. Some XENON100 project members have joined PandaX. Others signed on to the LUX project in South Dakota. That is partially funded by the DOE—for now. Big budget cuts in the near future might jeopardize many of the U.S. government's planned scientific projects.

Astrophysicist Stefan Funk, who searches for dark matter indirectly by scanning the heavens for gamma rays, told *Nature* magazine in February 2013, "Spending all our money on different direct-detection experiments is not worth it." However, there are others in the field who feel that competitionwill drive research teams to improve the quality of their equipment and ultimately benefit the dark matter search.

New Directions

In a March 2014 article for *Nature*, astrophysicist Mario Livio and astronomer Joe Silk called for the scientific community to refocus its efforts to unlock dark matter's mysteries. They pointed out that even some of the most respected, well-funded, and advanced efforts at finding WIMPs have not yet turned up any definitive proof, despite many years of research. Livio and Silk called for researchers to consider different particles. They also urged experimental methods.

"More varied particle types should be sought. Definitive tests need to be devised to rule out some classes of dark matter and some theories. If dark matter remains undiscovered in the next decade, then physicists will have to seriously reconsider alternative theories of gravity." Livio and Silk suggested that the various WIMP-hunting projects should expand their horizons to consider larger particles than the light WIMPs most are currently looking for. They also pointed out that it might take detectors one hundred times larger than the one in the LUX to get conclusive evidence of WIMPs.

THE SEARCH CONTINUES...

For better or for worse, the search for dark matter continues. Scientists worldwide are mostly convinced that the quest will be a fruitful one. Even if theories are turned upside down in the process or scientists must drastically revamp their ideas about what dark matter might be, science and humanity are sure to benefit.

For the astronomers, astrophysicists, and particle physicists hot on the trail of dark matter's secrets, the road to knowledge is as satisfying and inspiring as the knowledge itself. As Vera Rubin wrote, "We have peered into a new world and have seen that it is more mysterious and more complex than we had imagined. Still more mysteries of the universe remain hidden. Their discovery awaits the adventurous scientists of the future. I like it this way."

1609 Galileo Galilei demonstrates one of his early telescopes. With it, he observes previously unseen stars and gets closer views of the moon and Jupiter's moons.

1905 Albert Einstein publishes his paper "On the Electrodynamics of Moving Bodies," which comes to be known as the Special Theory of Relativity.

1916 Einstein publishes "The Foundation of the Generalized Theory of Relativity," which becomes known as the General Theory of Relativity.

1932 Einstein and Dutch physicist and astronomer Willem de Sitter coauthor a paper that argues that there may be large amounts of matter that do not emit light.

1924–25 American astronomer Edwin Hubble publishes his findings that the universe includes galaxies outside of the Milky Way.

1927 Georges Lemaître, a Belgian priest and astronomer, becomes the first academic to propose the theory of the expansion of the universe.

1929 Edwin Hubble's observations confirm that the universe is expanding and includes galaxies outside of the Milky Way.

1932 Dutch astronomer Jan Oort posits the idea of dark matter when his measurements indicate that the mass in a galactic plane must be more than the material that can be seen.

1933 Swiss astrophysicist Fritz Zwicky finds evidence of unseen mass while studying the Coma cluster of galaxies. He infers that there must be nonvisible matter present to provide enough mass and gravity to hold the cluster together.

1936 In studying the Virgo cluster of galaxies, American astronomer Sinclair Smith concludes that a large amount of invisible matter holds the galaxies together.

1939 American astronomer Horace Babcock's doctoral thesis includes one of the earliest indications of dark matter. His measurements indicate a growing mass-to-luminosity ratio in the outer portions of the Andromeda galaxy. He does not suspect the presence of unseen matter, however, but rather the absorption of light within the galaxy.

1949 English astronomer Fred Hoyle coins the term the "big bang" but later disavows the theory. He agrees that the universe is expanding but feel it is eternal—in a "steady state"—and has no beginning.

1959 German astrophysicist Franz Kahn and Dutch astronomer Lodewijk Woltjer suggest that invisible masses of hot gas exist within or between the Milky Way and Andromeda galaxies.

1965 Bell Labs physicist Arno Penzias and astronomer Robert Wilson discover cosmic microwave background (CMB) radiation. This is believed to be remnant or "leftover" radiation from the big bang.

1970s American astronomers Vera Rubin and W. Kent Ford's calculations indicate that galaxies must contain at least ten times as much dark matter as that provided by visible stars in order to achieve enough mass to avoid flying apart.

Late Bernard Sadoulet and Walter Stockwell of the
1980s Center for Particle Astrophysics set in motion
the Cryogenic Dark Matter Search (CDMS),
an experiment designed to detect WIMPs
(weakly interacting massive particles), which
are believed by some to be the major component of dark matter.

1993 Massive astrophysical compact halo objects,
or MACHOs, are theorized. Some physicists
believe these objects, which emit very little
light, account for much of the galactic mass
attributed to dark matter.

1994 American astrophysicist John Bahcall and
astronomer Andrew Gould study the Milky
Way's halo and conclude that brown and red
dwarfs—faint stars—account for only a rela-
tively small percentage of dark matter.

2000 Research teams studying MACHOs conclude
that they are not a major component of dark
matter.

2007 CDMS announces two "detections" but says
that these results cannot be interpreted as
"significant evidence for WIMP interactions."

2011 The Alpha Magnetic Spectrometer (AMS) is installed in low Earth orbit and is designed to detect evidence of dark matter.

2012 The Higgs boson particle—the so-called God particle—is discovered with the help of the Large Hadron Collider (LHC) in Geneva, Switzerland.

2014 In an article for *Nature*, astrophysicist Mario Livio and astronomer Joe Silk call for the scientific community to refocus its efforts to unlock dark matter's mysteries.

astrophysics The branch of physics that applies its laws to the study of stars and other celestial bodies.

black hole An extremely dense concentration of matter so powerful it sucks in other matter and light.

blueshift When an object's electromagnetic wavelength decreases. In astronomy, this indicates the object is moving toward the observer.

elusive Hard to detect, find, or figure out.

fluctuation An irregular rise or fall in the number of something, or a noticeable change in something.

gamma ray High-energy, radioactive photon.

gravitational microlensing Analyzing the light that is bent around a celestial object due to its gravity to gain details and information on that object's properties.

halo The roughly round outer part of a galaxy that extends beyond the visible part.

MACHO Massive astrophysical compact halo object; an astronomical object theoretically located in a galaxy halo that may be dark matter.

neutralino A hypothetical tiny particle that may be dark matter.

neutrino An elementary, tiny particle with zero charge.

particle physics The branch of physics that investigates the properties of extremely tiny particles and their roles in matter and the universe.

photon A tiny particle of light or electromagnetic radiation.

red dwarf A small, dim, faintly reddish star.

redshift When an object's electromagnetic wavelength increases. In astronomy, this indicates the object is moving away from the observer.

rotation curve A mapped curve that shows the differences in rotation speeds of celestial bodies in a certain place around a central point.

spectrometer Also known as a spectrograph, a tool used by astronomers to measure the light properties of distant celestial objects.

white dwarf An extremely dense but faint star.

WIMPs Weakly interacting massive particles; theorized tiny, unseen particles that may be dark matter.

xenon A heavy, colorless gas, often used in liquid form in dark matter experiments.

American Astronomical Society (AAS)
2000 Florida Avenue NW, Suite 300
Washington, DC 20009-1231
(202) 328-2010
Website: https://aas.org
The American Astronomical Society is a professional organization of astronomers and members in related fields, dedicated to promoting and advancing astronomy and the sciences in general.

Canadian Astronomical Society
National Research Council of Canada
5071 West Saanich Road
Victoria, BC V9E 2E7
Canada
(250) 363-6925
Website: http://casca.ca
The Canadian Astronomical Society is a society of professional astronomers, with membership open to anyone with a professional involvement in astronomy and related disciplines, that supports the scientific activities and its members and promotes the advancement of science in Canada and worldwide.

Department of Earth, Atmospheric, and Planetary Sciences
Massachusetts Institute of Technology
77 Massachusetts Avenue
Cambridge, MA 02139
(617) 253-2127

Website: http://eapsweb.mit.edu
The Massachusetts Institute of Technology's Department of
Earth, Atmospheric, and Planetary Sciences maintains one of
the most respected reputations for astronomical research in the
United States.

Fermilab
U.S. Department of Energy
P.O. Box 500
Batavia, IL 60510-5011
(630) 840 3000
Website: https://www.fnal.gov
Founded in 1967, Fermilab is the U.S. Department of Energy's
high-energy physics research lab dedicated to scientific advances
in figuring out how the universe works, including seeking out the
nature of dark matter and dark energy.

Hayden Planetarium/American Museum of
Natural History
81 Central Park West
New York, NY 10023
(212) 769-5100
Website: http://www.amnh.org/our-research/
hayden-planetarium
The Hayden Planetarium at the American Museum of Natural
History aims to bring new and historical information about astrophysics to the public via exhibitions and online resources and
programming.

National Aeronautics and Space Administration (NASA)
300 E Street SW
Washington, DC 20546
(202) 358-0000
Website: http://www.nasa.gov
The National Aeronautics and Space Administration is the top U.S. federal agency for civilian space exploration and aerospace research.

Royal Astronomical Society of Canada (RASC)
203-4920 Dundas Street West
Toronto, ON M9A IB7
Canada
Website: http://www.rasc.ca
The Royal Astronomical Society of Canada is a nonprofit organization of professionals, educators, and amateur astronomers, with twenty-nine branches around Canada.

WEBSITES

Because of the changing nature of Internet links, Rosen Publishing has developed an online list of websites related to the subject of this book. This site is updated regularly. Please use this link to access the list:

http://www.rosenlinks.com/PHYS/Dark

Anderson, Michael. *Pioneers in Astronomy and Space Exploration* (Inventors and Innovators). New York, NY: Rosen Educational Services, 2012.

Asimov, Isaac. *Asimov on Astronomy.* New York, NY: Bonanza Books, 1988.

Baxter, Roberta. *The Particle Model of Matter* (Sci-Hi: Physical Science). North Mankato, MN: Sci-Hi, 2009.

Bortz, Fred. *The Big Bang Theory: Edwin Hubble and the Origins of the Universe* (Revolutionary Discoveries of Scientific Pioneers). New York, NY: Rosen Publishing Group, 2014.

Dufay, Jean. *Introduction to Astrophysics: The Stars* (Dover Books on Physics). Mineola, NY: Dover Publications, 2012.

Graham, Ian. *What Do We Know About the Solar System?* (Earth, Space & Beyond). North Mankato, MN: Raintree, 2011.

Grayson, Robert. *Exploring Space* (The Story of Exploration). North Mankato, MN: ABDO Publishing Company, 2014.

Gregersen, Erik, ed. *The Britannica Guide to Particle Physics* (Physics Explained). New York, NY: Rosen Educational Services, 2011.

Haerens, Margaret, ed. *NASA* (Opposing Viewpoints). Farmington Hills, MI: Greenhaven Press, 2012.

Haugen, David M., ed. *Space Exploration* (At Issue). Farmington Hills, MI: Greenhaven Press, 2011.

Hawking, Stephen. *A Brief History of Time.* St. Louis, MO: Turtleback Books, 1998.

Hawking, Stephen. *The Universe in a Nutshell.* New York, NY: Bantam Books, 2001.

Hollar, Sherman, ed. *Astronomy: Understanding the Universe* (Solar System). New York, NY: Rosen Educational Services, 2011.

Miller, Ron. *Recentering the Universe: The Radical Theories of Copernicus, Kepler, Galileo, and Newton.* Minneapolis, MN: Lerner Publishing Group, 2013.

Moche, Dinah L. *Astronomy: A Self-Teaching Guide* (Wiley Self-Teaching Guides). Hoboken, NJ: Wiley, 2009.

Morris, Neil. *What Does Space Exploration Do for Us?* (Earth, Space & Beyond). North Mankato, MN: Raintree, 2011.

Scientific American. *Beyond Extreme Physics* (Cutting-Edge Science). New York, NY: Rosen Publishing Group, 2008.

Snedden, Robert. *How Do Scientists Explore Space?* (Earth, Space & Beyond). North Mankato, MN: Raintree, 2011.

Topp, Patricia. *This Strange Quantum World and You.* Grass Valley, CA: Blue Dolphin Publishing, 2013.

Tyson, Neil deGrasse. *Space Chronicles: Facing the Ultimate Frontier.* New York, NY: W. W. Norton & Company, 2013.

American Museum of Natural History. "Vera Rubin and Dark Matter." Amnh.org. Retrieved July 30, 2014 (http://www.amnh.org /education/resources/rfl/web/essaybooks /cosmic/p_rubin.html).

Aron, Jacob. "Did Dark Matter Kill the Dinosaurs? Maybe..." *New Scientist*, March 6, 2014. Retrieved March 9, 2014 (http://www .newscientist.com/article/dn25177-did-dark -matter-kill-the-dinosaurs-maybe.html# .UxyWE_0rvR1).

Bortz, Fred. *The Big Bang Theory: Edwin Hubble and the Origins of the Universe.* New York, NY: Rosen Publishing Group, 2014.

Byrne, Michael. "Astronomer Stacy McGaugh on a Universe Without Dark Matter." *Vice*, March 2, 2011. Retrieved March 18, 2014 (http://motherboard.vice.com/blog/q-a -astronomer-stacy-mcgaugh-on-a-dark-matter -less-universe).

Cartlidge, Edwin. "CoGeNT Gives Further Backing to Annual Dark-Matter Variation." Physicsworld.com, January 20, 2014. Retrieved March 14, 2014 (http://physicsworld.com /cws/article/news/2014/jan/20/cogent-gives -further-backing-to-annual-dark-matter -variation).

Cho, Adrian. "More Evidence Against Dark Matter?" *Science*, February 25, 2011. Retrieved January 27, 2014 (http://news .sciencemag.org/physics/2011/02/more -evidence-against-dark-matter).

Choi, Charles Q. "Elusive Dark Matter May Have Already Been Found." Space.com, December 9, 2013. Retrieved January 10, 2014 (http:// www.space.com/23879-dark-matter-detection -discovery.html).

Encyclopædia Britannica. "Astrolabe." Retrieved April 4, 2014 (http://www.britannica.com/ EBchecked/topic/39959/astrolabe).

Garfinkle, David, and Richard Garfinkle. *Three Steps to the Universe: From the Sun to Black Holes to the Mystery of Dark Matter.* Chicago, IL: University of Chicago Press, 2008.

Gates, Evalyn. *Einstein's Telescope.* New York, NY: W. W. Norton & Company, 2010.

Gilster, Paul. "Ubiquitous Brown Dwarfs: A Dark Matter Solution?" Centauri Dreams, April 22, 2009. Retrieved February 1, 2014 (http://www .centauri-dreams.org/?p=7420).

Goldsmith, Donald. "Dark Matter." *Natural History Magazine*, 2008. Retrieved January 30, 2014 (http://www.naturalhistorymag.com/ features/011330/dark-matter).

Grossman, Lisa. "Big Bang Birthday: Six Mysteries of a Cosmic Bombshell." *New Scientist*, February 20, 2014. Retrieved March 10, 2014 (http://www.newscientist.com/article/dn25097 -big-bang-birthday-six-mysteries-of-a-cosmic -bombshell.html#.UyZHjVwrvR0).

Herman, Rhett, and Shane L. Marson. "Is Dark Matter Theory or Fact?" *Scientific American*, June 15, 1998. Retrieved January 20, 2014 (http://www.scientificamerican.com/article /is-dark-matter-theory-or).

Hubble, Edwin. *The Realm of the Nebulae*. New Haven, CT: Yale University Press, 2013.

Inskeep, Steve (host). "A Scientific Tour of the Mysterious 'Dark Universe.'" NPR *Morning Edition*, October 31, 2013. Retrieved February 27, 2014 (http://www.npr.org/templates/story/ story.php?storyId=242028462).

Jamieson, Valerie. "Second Experiment Hints at Seasonal Dark Matter Signal." *New Scientist*, May 3, 2011. Retrieved February 7, 2014 (http://www.newscientist.com/article/dn20434 -second-experiment-hints-at-seasonal-dark -matter-signal.html).

Livio, Mario, and Joe Silk. "Physics: Broaden the Search for Dark Matter." *Nature*, March 5, 2014. Retrieved March 15, 2014 (http://www

.nature.com/news/physics-broaden-the-search
-for-dark-matter-1.14795).

Matson, John. "Tweak Gravity: What If There
Is No Dark Matter?" *Scientific American,*
November 5, 2009. Retrieved January 22, 2014
(http://www.scientificamerican.com/article
/dark-matter-modified-gravity).

Matson, John. "WIMP Wars: Astronomers and
Physicists Remain Skeptical of Long-Standing
Dark Matter Claim." *Scientific American,* May
6, 2011. Retrieved March 2, 2014 (http://
www.scientificamerican.com/article/dama
-dark-matter).

Maurer, Stephen M. "Idea Man." *Beam Line,*
Winter 2001. Retrieved February 27, 2014
(http://www.slac.stanford.edu/pubs/beamline
/31/1/31-1-maurer.pdf).

MIT News. "CDMS Result Covers New Ground in
Search for Dark Matter." February 28, 2014.
Retrieved March 2, 2014 (http://web.mit.edu
/newsoffice/2014/cdms-result-covers-new
-ground-in-search-for-dark-matter.html).

Moskowitz, Clara. "Mysterious Invisible Galaxy
May Be Composed of Dark Matter." *Christian
Science Monitor,* January 19, 2012. Retrieved
February 20, 2014 (http://www.csmonitor.com
/Science/2012/0119/Mysterious-invisible
-galaxy-may-be-composed-of-dark-matter).

Nicholson, Iain. *Dark Side of the Universe: Dark Matter, Dark Energy, and the Fate of the Cosmos.* Baltimore, MD: Johns Hopkins University Press, 2007.

Palmer, Roxanne. "Neil deGrasse Tyson Narrates 'Dark Universe,' Chats About Dark Matter." *International Business Times*, October 28, 2013. Retrieved March 10, 2014 (http://www.ibtimes.com/neil-degrasse-tyson-narrates-dark-universe-chats-about-dark-matter-1444292).

Panek, Richard. "Dark Energy: The Biggest Mystery in the Universe." *Smithsonian Magazine*, April 2010. Retrieved January 17, 2014 (http://www.smithsonianmag.com/science-nature/dark-energy-the-biggest-mystery-in-the-universe-9482130).

Panek, Richard. *The 4 Percent Universe.* New York, NY: Houghton Mifflin Harcourt, 2011.

Powell, Corey S. "Inside the Hunt for Dark Matter." *Popular Science*, November 2013. Retrieved January 14, 2014 (http://www.popsci.com/article/science/inside-hunt-dark-matter).

Reich, Eugenie Samuel. "Dark-Matter Hunt Gets Deep." *Nature*, February 21, 2013. Retrieved February 1, 2014 (http://www.nature.com/news/dark-matter-hunt-gets-deep-1.12455).

Smith, Robert. *Expanding Universe.* New York, NY: Cambridge University Press, 2009.

Soter, Steven, and Neil deGrasse Tyson, eds. *Cosmic Horizons: Astronomy at the Cutting Edge.* New York, NY: The New Press, 2000.

Spotts, Peter N. "Whatever Universe Is, Here's What It Isn't." *Christian Science Monitor,* November 17, 1994. Retrieved March 10, 2014 (http://www.csmonitor.com/1994/1117 /17081.html).

Yale News. "Discovery Triples Numbers of Stars in Universe." December 1, 2010. Retrieved January 30, 2014 (http://news.yale.edu /2010/12/01/discovery-triples-number-stars -universe).

ABOUT THE AUTHOR

Philip Wolny is a writer from Queens, New York. His other science-related titles for Rosen Publishing include *Chemical Reactions* (Science Made Simple) and *Isaac Asimov* (Great Science Writers).

PHOTO CREDITS